The Amazing Adventures of Awesome Amani

by

Jamiyl Samuels & Tracy-Ann Samuels

Illustrated by Israel Ramirez

DEDICATION

To our son Trey Amani Samuels
Thank you for being such a wonderful, caring, affectionate little boy
and for inspiring me to write this book.

Our daughter Aja
Thank you for being Trey's little sister and his mother. Your
existence has helped Trey on so many levels and inspired Book 2.

To the parents of children who are autistic or on the spectrum,
developmentally delayed, have attention deficit hyperactivity disorder
(ADHD) or communication disorders. Stay positive, stay strong,
provide your child with the help he/she needs early. God always
makes a way when it seems there is none.

ACKNOWLEDGMENTS

Israel Ramirez for coming through in the clutch with the amazing cover art and illustrations. Your hard work is very much appreciated.

To all the parents, doctors, therapists (speech, occupational, physical), teachers, teacher aides, and members of the Department of Education who are doing their part to assist children who are autistic, developmentally delayed, suffer from ADHD, communication and/or speech delays and more, I thank you for your service in improving the lives of the future of our country.

Special Thanks to:

The staff of Tiegerman Elementary and Middle School in Glen Cove, New York for allowing us to give back to you through these stories. Your tireless dedication to our HERO has made a world of difference.

Everyone who has supported *"The Amazingly Awesome Amani"* and *"The Amazingly Awesome Amani Takes On JITTERS & FEAR"* children's books. Thank you for supporting our movement to educate through awareness and entertain through pictures and words!

It is easy to envy what you perceive others to have, hard to see their struggle

CHAPTER 1

"Heellp!" "Heeellllp!"

The blood curdling shrieks startled seven-year old Amani Taylor. He arose from his deep sleep and turned his head to the bedroom window on his left.

He quickly throws the Ninja Mutant superhero sheets covering his tall, slim 60-pound frame back, takes a quick glance to his right at his younger sister Sandy, still comfortably resting under her own plush bed linens, and runs to the window to see what is happening.

The view from two stories below shows a middle-aged woman in distress, standing at the foot of a tall tree and looking towards the sky. Amani followed the woman's eyes and looked towards the top of the tree. In between the leaves and branches was a cat with light brown fur trying to balance on one of the limbs with its paws.

Amani wondered how the cat got in the tree. Suddenly, a gust of wind swept past causing the tree branches and leaves to move from side to side. This scared the cat who let out a cry as it tried to keep its balance. The lady gasped as she tried to move herself into a position to catch her beloved pet if it should lose its grip.

'There was no time to lose,' thought Amani.

Surely the cat would get seriously hurt if he did not act in a timely fashion. He took another glance at his sister who shifted ever so slightly under her Doctor Girl sheets yet was still clueless to the urgency of the moment.

Amani quickly ran into his closet and emerged with a jumpsuit made of blue fabric with an "A" hand painted in green on the chest. A red cape extended down his back to complete the outfit.

What seemed like a Halloween costume to the outside world was the uniform of a crime-fighting superhero! In a matter of seconds, a green mask with two holes cut into it was placed over his eyes with a rubber band and Awesome Amani was ready to save the day!

Another scream from the victim pierced the night air. Amani began to look around the room for anything he could use to save the feline. He darted to his toy box and began rummaging through the scores of action figures, toy cars, and other items.

Once satisfied with the tools in his arsenal, stuffed into a green and black book bag, Amani looked towards his bedroom door. He knew he could not go that way for fear of being seen by his Mommy and Daddy. The window was the only way to get outside.

"Someone help me, please!"

Amani made a mad dash to the window. Using both hands he slowly opened it while looking back at his sister, careful not to wake her. Putting the book bag on his back, he slid his right leg out turning sideways followed by his left. He shifted his body so that his back was facing the window as he slithered his upper body out. In one motion Amani let his lower body fall slowly out the window twisting his upper body so that his chest is facing the brick siding of the house.

With only his hands maintaining a tight grip on the window ledge, Amani pressed his toes against the side of the house and pushed back simultaneously releasing his fingers from the ledge. The approximately eight to ten-foot drop is a seamless one for him as he lands in the grass below without incident, making a swooshing noise to simulate the feeling that he was flying.

"Hold on, baby!" yelled the woman.

The wind was blowing harder now moving the tree at a speed that put the cat in danger. Amani had to think quickly. Slipping the bag off his shoulders, he zips it open and removes his little sister's jump rope.

Looking up at the tree, Amani held the rope in his right hand and bent his knees until he was very low to the ground. He threw one end of the rope towards the sky with all his might. The rope fell over one of the bigger limbs of the tree and fell back down to him.

Grabbing one end of the rope in each hand, Amani pulled himself up until his feet were off the ground. He relaxed his body and his feet came back to the concrete. The tree limb was strong enough to hold his weight.

Amani brought the two ends of the rope together in his hands and put his right foot on the tree. Pushing off on his right foot and pulling the rope at the same time, he began to climb the tree one step at a time. The cat turned slowly to face the person coming towards it.

As Amani got closer, he began talking to the cat.

"Hi, kitty. I'm coming to save you. Don't move," he whispered.

The cat gave a soft meow in return.

Amani got near enough to the cat to reach out and touch it, but he did not dare take his hands off the rope.

"Here kitty, kitty!" Amani called. The cat leaned forward, its nose moving quickly trying to pick up the scent of its rescuer.

"Go to the nice boy Precious," yelled the feline's owner from below.

"Yes, come to me Precious," Amani chimed in. He was desperate for the cat to move as he was losing his grip.

The cat seemed to trust Amani as it started to walk slowly toward him balancing its weight on the shaky branch.

"That's it. Come to poppa."

The cat crawled onto Amani's left shoulder.

"Good kitty. Hold on."

Amani began to climb down the tree one slow step at a time.

As he lowered himself down, his upper body would move causing the cat to shift slightly.

"Ouch!"

Naturally, the cat dug its sharp claws into Amani's shoulder so as not to lose its grip. It did not come this far to fall now. The cat's owner came closer to the tree excited to see her pet coming down to the ground.

When Amani got close enough, he pushed off the tree and landed on the ground. The cat leaped from his shoulders and into the lady's arms.

"Oh, thank you so much, young man," said the lady as she pulled her pet close to her body.

"You're welcome, ma'am," beamed Amani. "No problem at all."

Police and fire truck sirens began to wail in the distance. Someone else must have heard the woman's screams and called for help. As the noise grew louder, Amani looked back towards his house and noticed a light come on in the vicinity of his parent's bedroom.

Fresh beads of sweat appeared on Amani's forehead. A feeling of nervousness overcame him. He knew if he got caught outside after his bedtime, **he** would need an ambulance.

"H-Here you go," Amani stuttered in a fit of panic as he hurriedly stuffed the jump rope into his backpack.

"Oh my...," the confused woman uttered as Amani ran off in the direction he arrived.

In full sprint at this point, Amani managed to look back to make sure the authorities arrived to assist the woman. The perplexed look on the faces of the policemen and firemen as they scan the area for who or what scaled the tree to retrieve the cat causes him to smile.

As the grateful lady recounted her story to the authorities, Amani's focus returned to his house and the window he climbed out of. The commotion had awakened either his Mommy, Daddy, or both. If they were roused by the clamor, his parents would check on the children they believed were sleeping in their beds, not on the street in the middle of the night saving animals.

Amani had no time to lose. Just as he had helped the lady in distress, he would have to pull off the equally superhuman feat of getting back into his bedroom undetected.

As he arrived at the outside of his home there was one problem: he had jumped out of his window. He would have to find a way to get back up to his room. Nothing in his backpack of weapons and gadgets could help him climb the brick wall that separated the ground beneath him from the window.

The rope that was perfect for climbing the tree could not get him up a wall. He was not about to wake Sandy to ask her to hold the other end. That would be silly. She would not be able to hold his weight on the other end of the rope. He is too heavy for her five-year old body. Surely he would pull her out of the window. Plus, she would just tell on him rather than save him anyway.

Amani thought hard knowing he did not have much time. His parents were probably on the way to his bedroom. He looked at the cars parked in the driveway. One of the vehicles, a gray jeep, was parked just beneath the open window to the guest room.

The lightbulb going off in Amani's head was visible on his face. He ran to the front of the jeep and climbed on the hood. Reaching forward with both hands he grabbed the ends of the mounting rack on the roof of the vehicle and pulled himself up. At this height he was approximately a foot away from the window.

Amani braced himself and jumped into the air grabbing hold of the window ledge. Pressing his toes into the side of the building between two bricks, he was able to hold his weight as he used his left hand to quickly lift the mesh screen.

Amani swiftly returned his left hand to its place on the ledge before he lost his grip with the right hand. Placing the tips of his toes on the bricks, he pushed his weight upward and launched himself into the guest room window.

Landing on the full-size bed with his legs dangling from the window, Amani grabbed onto the edge of the bed and pulled himself completely into the room.

Lying on his stomach, Amani listens for any movement from his Mommy and Daddy. There is complete silence. Suddenly, a toilet flushes and he springs to his feet sprinting to the guest room door. He opens the door and peeks out into the hallway. He can see his room from where he is standing.

Unfortunately, the one door that lies between Amani and a successful return to his bed is the bathroom door. The sound of the flushing toilet subsides and there is a momentary silence. At any moment the door could swing open and it would be over. Awesome Amani would be caught red handed. Thinking about others would get him an other-worldly butt whipping.

At this point Amani was frozen with fear. So close, yet so far. Too afraid to make a dash for his bedroom as the creaky auburn-colored carpet would announce his steps like a rooster crowing at the rising sun.

So here it was, doomed to death by Caribbean punishment. Amani had to be thinking if it was worth it. The lady could have gotten another cat. He, however, would feel the lingering pain for his dangerous dalliance into the night.

Then, suddenly, a sound.

Amani's downtrodden mood suddenly dissipates. His shoulders, slumped in the inevitability of his fate, quickly straighten up. The water from the bathroom sink is running. And just like that, another chance.

'Thank goodness Mommy and Daddy washes their hands,' Amani thought.

After all, that is what they tell him and his sister to do every time he is done using the bathroom.

He sticks his right foot out the guest room into the hallway. Once his toes dig into the floor, a creaking noise stops his movement.

The water continues running and Amani realizes it is now or never. He takes four hurried tip-toed steps to his bedroom door. He quickly opens it and slides his body inside. Once on the other side of the door he holds the knob and twists it as he pushes it closed to mute any sound.

He made it!

Amani removed his backpack and climbed into his bed pulling the covers over his body just as the bedroom door opens. He turns his body on his left side unable to see who had come into the room.

"That's strange," Mommy said. "Why is the window open?"

Amani's eyes grow wide as he listened to his Mommy shut the window. As her steps grew closer, he quickly closes his eyes.

"Amani... Amani...," his Mom whispered as she gently nudged him.

'This was weird', Amani thought. Why was his Mommy trying to wake him up in the middle of the night?

Oh no! Amani suddenly realized he never removed his superhero suit before he climbed back into bed. It was too late now. His cover would be blown if he opened his eyes and got out of bed.

'Why wasn't Mommy waking Sandy up?' Amani thought.

"Amani!" The voice grew louder.

He was stuck. Keep his eyes closed and risk Mommy pulling the sheets away to make sure he gets out of bed or open his eyes and show her that he is awake and maybe she will leave the room.

The second option sounded like a plan. After taking a deep breath, Amani finally looked up.

He rubbed his face and looked at his Mommy standing over him. He turned his head towards the window and was shocked to see rays of sunlight streaming through.

"Get up," his Mommy urged. "You're going to be late for school!"

Amani heard birds chirping. The look of confusion on his face was apparent to his Mommy.

"That must have been some dream."

Amani peeked under his bed sheet. Still in his pajamas, he looked up at his Mommy and smiled widely showing his two new permanent front teeth separated by a slight gap.

CHAPTER 2

"Good morning Amani," Mommy said.

Amani smiled.

"Get up and use the bathroom and brush your teeth," Mommy continued. "Time to get ready for school."

Amani's expression quickly changed. It was the first day of school and he did not want to go. Mommy sat on his bed and slowly pulled the covers back.

"What's wrong, honey?" Mommy asked. "Are you scared?"

Amani nodded.

"It's okay to be nervous," Mommy smiled.

"Where's my big boy?" Daddy chimed in as he entered the room.

"Amani doesn't want to go to school," Mommy explained.

"Doesn't want to go to school?" Daddy repeated. "How do
you think Amazing Man became amazing?" Daddy said

pointing to the poster above Amani's bed of the superhero in the lime green jumpsuit with a dark green cape.

"There's nothing to be afraid of. Mommy and Daddy will be with you every step of the way," Mommy said.

Amani sat up in his bed.

"Remember, you can use your superpowers to calm those jitters," Daddy said pointing to Amani's superhero costume in his closet.

Amani immediately hopped out of the bed and started toward the closet.

"Amani," Mommy said. "That doesn't mean you can wear your costume to school."

Amani's smile instantly turned to a frown. It was like the wind was instantly let out of his sails, the air out of his tires.

"I think Daddy meant to use the superpowers in your mind," Mommy explained.

"Uh, yeah," Daddy said. "You have to wear regular clothes in school, son."

"Don't worry, baby. Halloween is right around the corner," Mommy said as she embraced Amani.

Amani headed to the bathroom to brush his teeth and wash his face. He had all right to be nervous. It was his fifth school in five years. Neither the private school, public school or

Catholic schools he attended during that time could effectively meet his needs.

Two years before, Amani was diagnosed with Autism Spectrum Disorder. More specifically, Mixed Receptive Language Disorder which made it hard for him to form complete sentences in response to others.

Although Amani is a shy child, he is very smart for his age. He started going to school at two years old. His pre-K-2 teacher always talked about how he knew all his shapes and letters of the alphabet. That came as no surprise to Daddy, as he always sang the alphabet song to him, especially when he would cry. Once Amani heard the melody of the letters A through Z, he would immediately stop crying.

His teacher would say Amani was very quiet. He played by himself and did not really talk to the other kids. Yet whenever Mommy or Daddy came to pick him up at the end of the day, he was always surrounded by three little girls in his class. One of the girls helped him put on his coat, another girl helped with his backpack, and the third little girl placed his lunchbox in his hand. All three then personally escorted him to his parents. Daddy got a kick out of this. His little boy was already a lady's man.

Amani was fascinated by computers, especially his Daddy's laptop, and was able to use it to find his favorite games and educational programs as a three-year old. 'This was amazing,' Mommy and Daddy thought. He used the computer better than his parents at times.

Mommy and Daddy noticed a change in Amani's behavior when speaking about his Pre-K-3 teacher. When dropping Amani at the school, she would show herself as nice and caring, but both parents discovered she was very mean. Amani was hesitant to go to the teacher and there were days he did not want to go to school at all.

Ultimately the decision was made to remove Amani from the school. He would spend the time at home with Daddy.

Amani had fun with Daddy during the day. They would watch cartoons together, play games on Daddy's laptop computer or make up games with Amani's toys. Although they were having a good time, Amani was still missing out on being around other kids. He spent all his time around adults.

Amani started a new school for pre-kindergarten. He seemed happy in his new surroundings. By the end of the first week he was able to tell Mommy and Daddy the name of his teacher: Ms. Kane.

A lot of Amani's responses were one-word answers. He often mimicked what he heard on television. At one point, a large portion of his speech was dialogue from shows like 'Yo Gabba Gabba' and 'Wow Wow Wubbzy!'

By the second week of school, Mommy and Daddy would ask Amani who was in his class. He was able to tell his parents the names of all his classmates. Surely Amani would be able to make new friends in this setting.

Amani loves music. Once he hears a favorite song he will rock from side to side. One morning he walked up to the ironing board and began touching it with his fingers as if he was playing the piano.

Amani also has a great voice. He would sing at random, mainly religious songs. He sang as he played his imaginary instrument.

"Did you learn those songs at school?" Mommy asked.

Amani nodded.

One morning Daddy took Amani to school and stayed to see how he was doing. At a certain time of the morning the kids would all line up and file out of their classrooms into an open space where there were seven to eight rows of chairs lined up for the kids to sit on.

A wooden piano sat at the front of the room to the left a few feet away from the chairs. As soon as it was 9 o'clock, children began walking out of their classrooms led by their teachers and filling in the seats with the smallest kids, the two-year olds, in the first two rows, the three-year olds behind them, and so on.

This gathering was a daily routine at the school called "chapel". It was reminiscent of a church service where the teachers led the children in songs and passages from the Bible.

Before chapel began, an older man with glasses dressed in a suit and tie sat on a small wooden stool in front of the piano and began to play. Daddy looked at Amani when the music began and saw a child fascinated by the way the man was moving his fingers across the keys. He noticed as the children sang Amani knew every single word. These were the songs Daddy was hearing Amani sing in the house.

After chapel was over the kids returned to their classrooms for the lessons of the day. Daddy asked Ms. Kane how Amani was doing in class.

"Let me show you some of his work," Ms. Kane said as she ran her thumb through a pile of folders.

Once she arrived at Amani's name, she pulled the folder out.

"I have no problem with Amani in regard to his behavior," the teacher continued pulling her glasses slightly down to look at Daddy.

"He is quiet," she continued. "He needs to participate more in class."

Ms. Kane opened the folder and pulled out a picture of a farm. There was a barn in the background. In the foreground was a picture of a pig in mud, on the opposite side were a group of chickens, and a cow near the barn with its head in the grass.

"I ask all the students to color a picture just to see where their skill level is," Ms. Kane said handing the picture to Daddy.

The entire page was colored in blue crayon outside of the lines. Daddy did not know what to think about what he was seeing. Ms. Kane showed him the same picture from a different student. A different color was used to represent each animal and the surrounding scenery.

"There is one child that sits directly across from Amani," she began. "He says Amani is always bothering him."

"Does the child talk to Amani?" asked Daddy.

"Yes, however, no matter what the child says Amani only smiles in return," offered Ms. Kane.

"He thinks Amani is laughing at him."

Daddy went home and shared this information with Mommy. All of Amani's teachers were saying the same thing about his lack of communication in school. Was this a cause for concern? Amani was only four years old.

"I was shy as a child," Daddy reasoned. "I didn't really start speaking in class until the third grade."

Daddy thought his son was following in his footsteps. That was a reasonable explanation. Kids usually fashion themselves in the image of their parents. However, Mommy's instincts told her something different. She had an idea that the way Amani colored was not appropriate. But he was still very young.

The following year Mommy and Daddy changed their living environment completely from renting a floor of a home in Brooklyn, New York to owning an entire house in Queens.

When Amani entered the new home for the first time he looked around. He knew something was different. The lack of furniture was the first clue.

"New house?" he managed to ask.

It was one of the rare times he put his thoughts into words at the appropriate time. The inquiry brought a smile to Mommy and Daddy's face.

"Yes, we are in a new house," Mommy said. "Do you like it?"

"Yes," Amani nodded.

Amani gave his stamp of approval which was huge for a child that did not respond well to change.

For Amani everything had to be the same all the time. His toys, especially his cars, had to be aligned just right. His books had to be stacked in a straight pile without a corner turned in a different direction. The tiny game cartridges for his hand-held learning device had to be set side by side with all the titles facing upwards.

Any sudden movement, act of nature, or accidental bumping of said items that jarred them out of uniformity would prompt swift action by Amani. Indecipherable mumbling would serve as the background noise as he returned the disturbed articles back to their rightful position.

Mommy noticed this behavior one too many times to not be bothered.

"That is not normal," she shared with Daddy.

"He just likes to keep his stuff in order," Daddy returned. "I wish I was that neat at his age."

The first night in his new bed, in his new room, in his new home, Amani laid in a bed made of blue plastic with the picture of a cowboy on the headboard and stared at the ceiling. He was tired from a long day of moving yet he was trying to fight the sleep. Still the darkness of the room was too inviting. His eyelids became heavy as if a fairy was tossing magic dust on them from huge sandbags. His pillow grew hands and started to massage the side of his head while his upper body sunk deeper into the feathery mattress beneath him.

Sleep was calling his name like a long-lost friend. Fatigue was winning the battle with stubbornness and Amani's eyes closed slowly and quickly opened again, his upper eyelids slid down a white eyeball river to meet its counterpart below for a split second and, just as suddenly, he was awake again. The red streaks of exhaustion stretched across the white of his optics pleading for closure. Then, once again, his eyes shut.

Amani's behavior began to change over the course of the next few months. He began to act out. There were angry outbursts seemingly out of nowhere. What Mommy and Daddy felt were insignificant issues would trigger violent temper tantrums.

Amani would cry at random moments during school nights, hours after he had arrived home. He still was not communicating in depth about how his day in school progressed, so his parents were left to wonder about the cause of these meltdowns.

Was the change in environment finally affecting him? Daddy was still commuting Amani to the school in Brooklyn. Maybe the thought of driving to Queens made him feel like he was leaving his home behind.

Was someone bothering him at school? When posed this question by Mommy and Daddy Amani did not illicit a response. It became frustrating not being able to get a clear understanding of the cause of Amani's distress, especially when the teacher was just as vague in her answers as Amani was.

Could Amani be jealous? At this point he was a big brother to his little sister Sandy for two years. Before then he had been the sole recipient of all the family's affection and adulation. The primary beneficiary of all toys, gifts, and other spoils of being a one of one.

Maybe he did not want to share anything or anyone he felt rightfully belonged to him. Sandy was using the wooden crib that once belonged to him. She was using some of his old toys and baby items.

Children are naturally territorial, selfish even, especially when they have been the center of attention. They must be taught to accept change, to share. They must know that they will not be treated differently. It is a lesson that is tough to adhere to in adults let alone a little boy.

When Sandy was born, Amani did not show any outward emotion. There were no fits of anger that would lead Mommy and Daddy to believe he was angry about sharing his parents.

On the contrary, Amani smiled at his baby sister as she lay in Mommy's arms in the hospital. Family members showered him with "awws" and other sounds of affection at the love fest they were witnessing.

For the rest of that summer the transition seemed effortless. Amani took every picture with his little sister with the pride only a big brother could have knowing he would be charged with protecting his younger sibling.

All was well.

CHAPTER 3

Amani sat down slowly at the lunch table. He looked to his left and then to his right. Some of the other kids were waiting for him to open his lunchbox to see what he had for lunch. He had a plan. He was going to wait until the lunchroom aide called his table. Once the other kids got up to get their trays, he would open his lunch and start eating.

Yeah.

That was the perfect plan.

"Open your lunchbox!" cried one little girl as she reached across Amani's body for his kit.

"No!" Amani yelled as he pulled back on the lunchbox. The two were engaged in an all-out tug of war as another little girl came over.

"Stop!" Amani yelled trying to get the attention of an adult in the cafeteria. There were lunch aides serving the trays in the kitchen, there were a few teachers around the massive space, but no one came to his rescue. Soon the two girls had their hands-on Amani's lunchbox trying to take it away.

"No!" Amani continued to yell. "Stop!"

"Amani!"

Amani looked around. It was his Daddy's voice, but Amani did not see him anywhere.

"Amani!"

Amani opened his eyes sat up and looked around. He saw his Daddy standing over his bed. He saw none of his classmates. He was in his bedroom.

"Are you alright, son?" Daddy asked. "Did you have a bad dream?"

Amani could not believe he was not at school.

"What were you dreaming about?"

Amani said nothing. Daddy sensed his son was in distress.

"Okay. Everything is fine now."

Daddy guided Amani's head down to his pillow. He pulled the covers up to Amani's neck and kissed his forehead.

As Daddy turned to leave Amani grabbed his arm. He did not want Daddy to go.

Daddy sighed and sat down on the bed.

"Listen, I don't know what has got you so scared, but nothing is going to hurt you while Mommy and Daddy is here. Okay?"

Amani nodded.

"And even when we are not here in the room with you..." Daddy continued as he stood up and walked toward the closet.

"Remember what you wore for Halloween?" Daddy asked.

Amani looked toward his closet as Daddy pulled out a blue jumpsuit with a red flowing cape.

"Whenever you feel afraid, just put on your costume and scare away those monsters!"

Amani looked at his Daddy and back at the costume.

"It will be right here," Daddy said as he placed the costume back in the closet.

"Do you want to stay in our room?" Daddy asked.

Amani nodded and climbed out of the bed.

These outbursts were becoming a regular occurrence over the past few weeks. To say Mommy and Daddy were worried would be an understatement.

In the fall, Mommy and Daddy made the decision to put Amani in a public school in Queens. Driving back and forth between boroughs was becoming a chore especially with another infant in the home. Amani had always attended private school, and this would be yet another change. Public school was not the ideal option, but it was decidedly less expensive. It was an easy choice to make.

Public school was a different entity altogether. Amani was behaving much differently than in previous years at private school. It was after a few weeks that his kindergarten teacher Ms. Daye started to voice concerns about his behavior. She did not sugarcoat what was happening in her classroom, candor that Mommy and Daddy needed from other teachers.

Both parents were shocked to learn what was taking place in Ms. Daye's class. According to the teacher, Amani would not stay in his seat during lessons. Instead he would walk around the room and laugh to himself. He also needed assistance putting on his jacket and schoolbag at the end of the day.

This was strange to Mommy and Daddy because Amani knew how to put on his clothes at home. That he had difficulty remaining seated was a relatively new challenge never divulged by his former teachers. Since Daddy was home during school hours it was decided that he would set up a time and day to observe Amani in the classroom.

Observations were scheduled by the school in conjunction with the parents to view their child in real time without the child's knowledge. This way Daddy can see for himself what Ms. Daye had been saying.

It was an ordinary Tuesday morning. Daddy dropped Amani at the same place he did every morning. This time Daddy could come inside.

Amani was a little surprised, but happy that Daddy was walking up the stairs with him. Once on the second floor Amani made a right turn. Daddy followed content to let his son lead the way.

Amani arrived at the classroom as the kids were removing their coats. Daddy greeted all of them. Amani seemed comfortable around his classmates so far.

"Good morning, Mr. Taylor," Ms. Daye smiled.

"Good morning."

Ms. Daye leaned over to Amani.

"Hello, Amani," she said, a hint of a Caribbean accent as she spoke.

Amani smiled and waved at Ms. Daye. She was a slight African American woman of medium height. Streaks of gray lined her black hair. She seemed very pleasant.

"Come children, it's time for circle time."

The kids all came together in a designated area of the class and formed a circle. This was a daily routine where the kids would clap their hands while each child would say his or her name. Amani seemed enthusiastic about this exercise.

"My name is Amani," he said as he smiled and clapped his hands.

Once every child had a turn, it was time to gather around Ms. Daye near the classroom library for story time.

"Ok, Amani. Daddy's gonna go now," Ms. Daye said.

Daddy took his cue to make himself scarce. He was not leaving the building, only the classroom where he would stand outside the door and watch Amani.

The class library has about five medium-sized wooden shelves filled with children's books. The shelves formed a semi-rectangle around the area which helped to separate it from the rest of the room.

Daddy looked through the glass square of the door and could see everything. He was also able to hear what Ms. Daye was saying to the kids.

As Ms. Daye began to read, Daddy watched as Amani rose to his feet and began walking back and forth in the library area. He wasn't looking at any books just moving around an imaginary track with a smile on his face.

Ms. Daye continued reading to the other children undeterred as if this was no surprise to her. Amani completely tuned out what was happening around him.

Daddy wondered why Amani wasn't paying attention. He continued to watch as Ms. Daye attempted to bring Amani back to the group.

"Have a seat Amani," Ms. Daye said as the other kids looked on. Some of them laughed while others looked at Amani strangely.

Amani returned to the group.

"Sit here in front of me," Ms. Daye offered.

Amani sat in front of his teacher with his legs crisscrossed and his hands on his lap.

Ms. Daye began to read again. Amani started to rock back and forth. A few of the other kids snickered as the movement continued. Amani looked around at the kids who were laughing and smiled at them.

"Amani, would you like to read the rest of the story?" Ms. Daye asked.

Amani nodded and took the book from Ms. Daye. He began to read every word aloud without hesitation, something most of the kids could not do. Once Amani finished, Ms. Daye led the class in applause.

Daddy walked away from the classroom door to look at the artwork posted on the wall. Many of Amani's drawings were of a boy drawn as a stick figure with a triangle shape extending from his back. It was a cape. What an imagination.

At lunchtime the kids all left the classroom and walked down two flights of stairs before they arrived at the cafeteria. Daddy had already made his way in and seated himself at a different table out of view of Ms. Daye's class.

Lunchtime for the kids meant break time for Ms. Daye. There were lunch aides and other teachers scattered around the cafeteria. However, they were nowhere near Ms. Daye's class as other students were entering the lunchroom.

Daddy watched as Amani sat down with his lunchbox. Each class had to wait to be called to receive their school lunch. Since Amani already had his food, he was the first to eat, or so Daddy thought.

As soon as Amani opened his lunchbox and the other kids saw the snacks he had, some of the girls slid over next to him.

"I want that," one girl said as she reached for Amani's cookies.

"Give me this," another girl yelled as she grabbed his fruit.

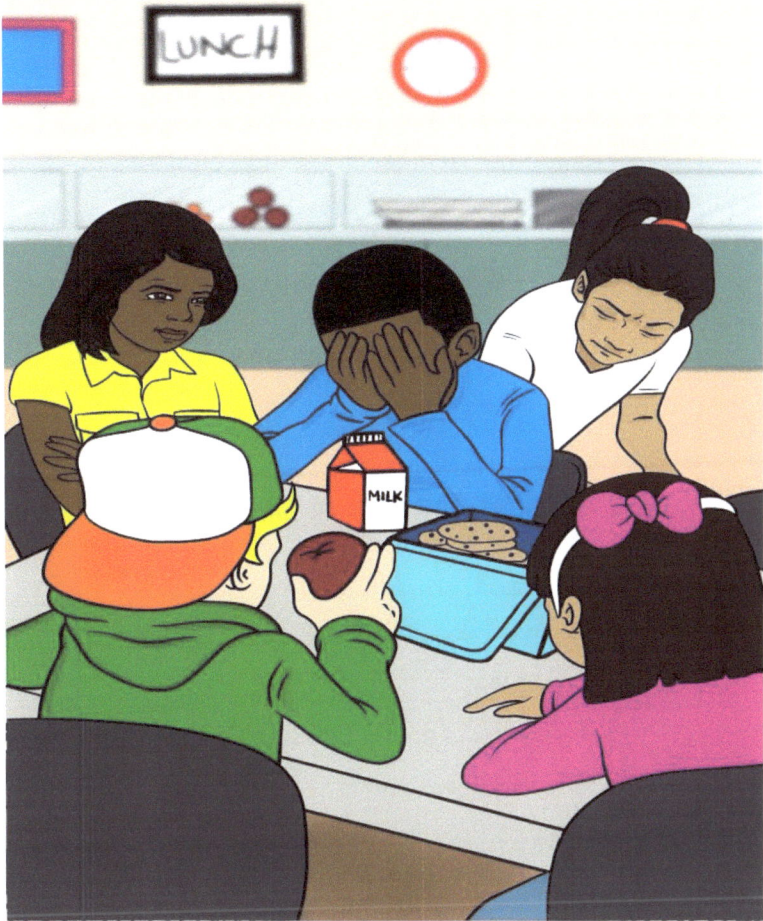

Daddy watched in utter disbelief as those kids began taking Amani's food right out of his lunchbox. Amani was visibly upset with what was happening, but he could not find the words to say what he was thinking.

Daddy looked around for the teachers, but no one was paying attention. The little girls moved in with such calculated precision that Daddy had to wonder if this was a regular occurrence. Either way, he was not about to stand by and watch these little girls take Amani's food, especially when they are about to eat the school lunch.

Daddy walked over to the table and reached over Amani taking the cookies and fruit away from each girl before they could open it.

"That's not yours," Daddy told the girls in a sing-song voice that masked his building anger.

He put the snacks back in Amani's lunchbox. The girls were not happy.

"You don't belong here," one of the girls snapped at Daddy.

"Well, I'm here today," Daddy said shocked at the response. "You have to ask for things nicely, you don't just take it."

He could not believe the audacity of these little girls. If this was happening to Amani every day, it was no wonder he was lashing out and having nightmares.

CHAPTER 4

Amani sat up in his bed. For some reason he could not sleep. He pulled his cover away from his body and got out of bed. He walked out of his bedroom, past the bathroom and guest room to Mommy and Daddy's room. He pushed the door open and looked in. Both parents were sound asleep. Amani slowly closed the door and headed back to his room.

Once inside Amani gently closed the door and walked towards his bed. After climbing into bed and sliding his feet under his covers, Amani laid on his left side, his left ear and cheek disappearing into the soft pillow, and slowly closed his eyes.

"Hey give that back!"

The noise put a wrinkle in Amani's face. He kept his eyes closed.

"Stop playing around!" yelled the same voice.

Amani opened his eyes this time and looked around. His window was closed yet the sound was as clear as if the person was lying right next to him. Wherever the voice was, that person was really in trouble.

Amani rose from his bed and darted to the window. He looked out and saw two boys arguing. One boy was bigger in size than the other. It looked like they were fighting over a bag.

"Let it go! It's mine!" yelled the smaller kid as he pulled on the bag.

Amani made up his mind that he was going to help, but he could not go outside in his pajamas. It was also past his bedtime. He could not afford to be seen by anyone that would tell his Mommy and Daddy. What was he going to wear? If he was going to save the day, he needed to dress the part. He looked up at the poster of Amazing Man. His costume was all green.

Amani did not have anything resembling a green costume, but he did have a Halloween outfit that just so happened to have a cape. He ran to his closet, grabbed the blue and red superhero suit and put it on quickly. Looking down at himself he noticed the "S" on his chest. He would have to change it to an "A" to match the first letter of his name.

"Give that back!"

There was no time to worry about letters. Amani ran back to the window and saw the two kids in an old-fashioned tug-of-war over the bag.

Amani had to do something. There was one problem. How was he going to get outside? He could not jump out of the window. He turned to his bedroom door and slowly walked towards it watching his little sister Sandy the entire time.

Once at the door, Amani slowly turned the knob and peeked out. There was complete silence from across the hall where Mommy and Daddy's room was, so he took a step out onto the red carpet with his right foot.

"CREEEAAAK!"

Amani was frozen as the creaky hardwood under the carpet sounded like a bomb going off in a library. He stood still for about five seconds listening for any movement from his parents' room. He heard nothing. He decided to take another step towards the staircase. His left foot produced silence. The carpet did its job under that foot.

Reaching for the bannister, Amani picked up his right and put it down on the top step.

"CRREEAAKK!"

That darn right foot did it again! Amani stopped as if he were touched by the "it" player in Freeze Tag. Again, he listened. Not a sound from the grownups. Still holding on to the bannister, Amani pulled his left leg onto the second step. There was a slight murmur, but nothing like the noise caused by his right foot. There were ten steps left to get to the bottom of the staircase. What was he going to do?

Amani moved his right foot down to the next step, but instead of placing his entire foot down he used his toes. It worked!

The toes on his right foot did not make a sound, so Amani went the rest of the way down the stairs with his left foot down and his right foot on his tip toes. He ran to the front door and quietly exited the house.

Once outside, Amani ran around to the back of the house. The two kids were still tussling over the bag a few yards away.

As Amani moved closer, the bigger kid had finally wrestled the bag away and began a mad dash in the opposite direction.

It reminded Amani of the kids in his kindergarten class that tried to take his lunch. He could not let someone else get away with taking something that was not theirs.

Amani had to think quickly. He looked around the area and saw his soccer ball sitting in the grass. It was slightly smaller than the regulation size used in his weekly intramural soccer games, but it was still something. Amani steadied the ball with his right foot while watching the bully run away. He brought his right leg back as far as he could and kicked the soccer ball hard in the direction of the fleeing bully.

The ball hit the intended target, lodging itself between the legs of the big kid in full stride. A violent collision between the bully's upper body and the concrete below him sent the bag hurtling through the air, finally landing a few feet away from the crumpled thief. The smaller kid, stunned at the sudden turn of events, stopped in his tracks and did not move until Amani ran by him.

The bully, not knowing what hit him, audibly groaned as he remained in a heap on the ground. Amani moved towards the bag and picked it up. The smaller kid finally made his way over to Amani.

"Here you go", Amani smiled.

"Thank you", the smaller kid said.

Satisfied that he was able to help, Amani began to walk away.

"Wait!" the kid shouted.

Amani turned around.

"What's your name?"

"Amani".

The kid smiled. "You're AWESOME," he gushed.

Amani smiled and turned toward his house, pleased by what he had accomplished. Happy that he was able to help someone who was in danger.

Amani's feel-good moment did not last long. He realized someone else needed help: himself. He would be in danger if he did not get back in his house before Mommy and Daddy woke up. He started running, passing the cars in the driveway. He made a left turn and made it the front of the house.

The next time someone needed his help, he would have to figure out an easier way to get outside. He most definitely could not keep going out the front door.

CHAPTER 5

Amani, Mommy, Daddy and Sandy arrived at his new school. It was a huge building with a large letter "T" colored blue surrounded by a gold circle high above the front entrance. There were several yellow school buses packed with kids parked along the curb leading to the front entrance. As the kids got off the bus, Amani noticed the ones who looked scared were being followed by a tall mean-looking person with a long, dark coat and hat.

"We are here," Daddy said. "Let's go inside."

As the family walked into the school Amani and Sandy immediately looked around. To the left was an office where two ladies sat behind a desk. The phones in front of them were ringing off the hook. To the right was a door made of hardwood. There was a nameplate on the door that said "Principal".

The door suddenly opened and an older woman with blond hair walked out. The woman did not immediately see the Taylor family as she exited her office, but as she proceeded to adjust her black sport coat it was clear she was getting ready to personally greet all who arrived through the main entrance.

"Good morning," the woman said as she looked to her left spotting the Taylor's. "I'm Mrs. Katz, the principal of Teague Elementary School."

Mrs. Katz extended her hand.

"Nice to meet you," Mommy said. "This is Amani."

Mrs. Katz leaned forward. "Well hello, Amani," she said shaking his hand.

Amani smiled nervously. Suddenly he saw two tall, shadowy figures rising behind Mrs. Katz. There were words on each of their chests. One read "JITTERS" and "FEAR" was emblazoned on the other. The eyes and mouth on one of them was bright red, as if it were bleeding. While the other was orange like fire. Amani was horrified as he watched the two sinister characters move closer to Mrs. Katz with their arms outstretched. Their mouths were open, and their eyes were narrow. They made the scariest face Amani had ever seen!

Amani was afraid they were going to hurt Mrs. Katz. He nervously pointed his finger in the direction of the two and closed his eyes. Mrs. Katz turned around.

"Oh, that is a portrait of the founder of our school Dr. Teague," Mrs. Katz explained.

Amani opened his eyes. The two figures had magically disappeared. There was only a huge picture frame of a woman with strawberry blond hair smiling.

Amani was confused. He looked at Mommy and Daddy to see if they saw what he had seen. He even looked at Sandy who was focused on her baby doll.

"Let me take you to the classroom," Mrs. Katz said.

Mommy, Daddy and Sandy turned left and followed Mrs. Katz. Amani walked up to the portrait to take a second look. Suddenly JITTERS and FEAR began to move towards him from the right. Amani ran to catch up with his family.

Mrs. Katz opened the door to classroom 310. A woman, standing near the front of the classroom looked over and smiled.

"This is Ms. Carulli," Mrs. Katz said. "She will be Amani's teacher."

"Please call me Ms. Cee," the teacher said as she approached the doorway.

Ms. Cee greeted everyone with a huge smile. Amani took a peak past Ms. Cee into the classroom. At the back of the room he saw two students frozen as FEAR stood over them. He looked back at Ms. Cee and saw JITTERS standing behind her.

"It's great to meet you Amani," Ms. Cee smiled. "We're going to have so much fun." She had no idea JITTERS was right behind her.

Suddenly, just as quickly as it appeared, JITTERS disappeared.

Ms. Cee took Amani by the hand and began to walk with him.

"Let's take a look around the room."

Ms. Cee showed Amani the library wall with different books. There was a play area with different toys. Amani liked this section a lot. As they continued around the room, Ms. Cee and Amani approached the two boys in the back of the room. FEAR began to go away as Ms. Cee moved closer to them.

"Amani, I would like you to meet Chris and Kyle," Ms. Cee said. "Boys, meet Amani."

Chris, a slim Caucasian boy, had brown floppy hair. Kyle was also slim with brown skin. He was taller than both Chris and Amani. His hair was cut low. Both boys smiled nervously at Amani.

"Are you boys okay?" Ms. Cee asked.

Both Chris and Kyle looked around before smiling.

"Don't worry. You boys are going to be great friends," Ms. Cee said. "You all get to know each other while I speak to Amani's Mommy and Daddy.

Ms. Cee walked away leaving all three boys and Sandy in the room. Not wanting to deal with stinky boys, Sandy walked over to the play area. Amani sat in a chair near Chris and Kyle. No one said a word. Amani decided to put his head down on the table until Ms. Cee came back. He was still a little tired from Mommy waking him up so early.

Once Ms. Cee left the room, JITTERS and FEAR reared their ugly heads once more. Chris and Kyle were very afraid. Amani picked his head up and saw the two fiends. He had just about enough of these shifty characters.

Amani stood up and tore open his shirt to reveal a green "A" on his chest. Chris and Kyle stared in disbelief as Amani ripped off his pants and stood in his full superhero suit. Awesome Amani was here to save the day!

"It's time for you to go!" Amani shouted at JITTERS and FEAR.

Suddenly Chris and Kyle became more confident knowing they had a superhero in their presence. They stood up out of their seats as well. They too would face down JITTERS and FEAR and drive them away for good!

Chris and Kyle stood on each side of Amani. Amani looked to his left and right, surprised that he had back up. All three boys began to walk towards JITTERS and FEAR.

"You don't stand a chance, JITTERS and FEAR!" Amani proclaimed! "Get out of this classroom!"

JITTERS and FEAR, no longer able to scare the boys, began to retreat. They were no match for Awesome Amani and his two classmates, so they took off. Sandy, hearing her brother yelling, looked up from the play area and saw him.

"Wow! You're AWESOME!" yelled Chris to Amani.

"That's my name," Amani began. "AWESOME AMANI!" "But I couldn't have done it without you two!" he continued.

"Really?!" Kyle asked.

"Yep! You guys were not going to let jitters and fear take over you," Amani explained.

"That was so cool how you ripped off your uniform and came out in your costume!" Chris beamed.

"Thanks," Amani said with a smile.

"MOM! DAD!"

Amani turned frantically in the direction of the scream. Sandy was running to the door of the classroom to tell Mommy and Daddy! They couldn't see him like this! He was told not to wear his superhero suit to school. There was no time to change back into his regular clothes. What was he going to do?

Amani sat up in his chair.

"Wake up, sleepy head," Mommy said.

Amani looked up and saw Mommy and Daddy surrounding him. He quickly looked down at his body and noticed he still had on his school clothes.

"Were we gone that long?" Daddy asked smiling.

"Leave my baby alone," Mommy said. "He woke up very early this morning."

Amani had fallen asleep at his desk.

"I think you're really going to love this school Amani," Daddy said. "It is extraordinary."

"We teach the extraordinary," Ms. Cee said.

Amani got out of his seat and walked over to Chris and Kyle. He gave them both a high five. The boys smiled at Amani. This was going to be the beginning of a great friendship.

The difference in Amani was noticeable right away after just one week of attending The Teague School. The teachers gave him a lot of attention, especially the one that came to see him to work on his speech.

Ms. Santana entered the classroom at a specific time each day and took Amani to a different room. There he worked on speaking in complete sentences, answering "w-h" questions like where, what, why, when, and reading comprehension where he would read a short story and then answer four to five questions about it.

Amani does not have any trouble reading. He had been doing so since he was a one-year old. Mommy and Daddy made sure he was being read to even before he was born. At two he was reading children's books by himself.

Another one of his teachers was fun to be around. Ms. Berger also removed Amani from his classroom three times a week and took him to another room where she helped strengthen the use of his hands. She also showed him the proper way to use scissors.

Now he can do class projects and homework that require cutting out animals and gluing it onto construction paper. He can cut shapes on a line and paste it to blank paper. He can even tie his shoelaces on his own, a task he was so excited about learning that he came home and showed Mommy and Daddy how to tie all his sneakers, shoes, and even the strings on his shorts.

Ms. Berger helped Amani with his handwriting by giving him sentences to copy. She worked on his spacing between words and placing punctuations at the end of his sentences with more regularity. She helped him remember that a capital letter begins every sentence as does the name of a person and place.

Most importantly, Amani wanted to go to school every day. He got up out of bed as soon as Mommy or Daddy told him it was time. The Teague School was everything the Taylors hoped for.

CHAPTER 6

Every night at 8 o'clock Amani knew it was time to get ready for bed. That meant taking a shower. Amani recently stopped taking baths and started showering on his own. This was a major milestone because Mommy or Daddy used to soap him up and he almost became dependent until one day Mommy gave him his own wash rag and showed him how to put soap on it and then rub it on his skin.

It did not take long before Amani started taking showers by himself. He always had the ability to learn quickly. Once he was done in the bath, he put on his favorite pajamas. He brushed his teeth and gargled with mouthwash to keep those nasty cavities away. Before he laid down to sleep, Amani knew he had to say his prayers.

He knelt by his bed, put his two hands together and closed his eyes.

"Our Father who art in heaven..." he began.

Once he finished his prayers, Amani climbed into his bed. This version was made of wood. He was a big boy now.

"Good night, son", Mommy said as she kissed Amani's forehead.

"Good night", Amani returned.

He pulled the Ninja Mutant covers up to his neck and closed his eyes. Mommy looked over at Sandy, who was already asleep, before quietly walking out of the room. Amani slowly shut his eyes.

"Woof! Woof!"
"Arf! Arf!"
"Bark! Bark!"

Amani's face wrinkled with discomfort at the sounds he was hearing. He tried to keep his eyes closed, but the constant barking was too much to bear. He opened his eyes as the noise got louder. It sounded like a bunch of angry dogs.

Amani ran to his window expecting to see at least four canines and was shocked to see only one. The dog was on a leash that was tied to a fence a few doors away. It was a beautiful little black Dachshund dog that seemed anxious as it struggled to free itself, even biting the leash at times to no avail.

Amani quickly ran to his closet and in a matter of seconds re-emerged as **AWESOME AMANI**. His bag of gadgets was securely on his back as he approached the window.

This time Amani made sure getting out the window would not be an issue as he picked up Sandy's jump rope. He tied one end to the leg of his dresser drawer affixed against the wall near the window. With both hands on the rope, Amani tested the line the only way he knew how – launching himself out of the window.

Success! The drawer never moved, its contents much heavier than Amani's body weight, and the hero was safely on the ground.

Amani knew he had to approach slowly. He looked around to see if there was anyone in the immediate area that would claim the dog. There was no one around.

"Here, boy!" Amani offered.

The dog turned to Amani and began barking at him. Amani jumped back as the dog continued to bark wildly. It started chewing on its leash again.

"Okay, take it easy," Amani pleaded. "I'm here to help you."

Amani had to think quickly. He reached into his backpack and pulled out a white Styrofoam carton.

"I don't have any doggie treats," Amani said as he pushed the carton towards the dog. "It's left over from my dinner."

The dog stopped barking and moved towards the carton of food.

"It's white rice and curry chicken. My favorite."

The dog's nose began moving at a rapid pace as it inched closer to the food placed in front of it. Within seconds the dog devoured the food, licking the empty container.

"Wow, you were hungry," Amani said as he moved towards the pooch.

Amani noticed the dog did not bark at him anymore, even as he moved closer to it. As he crouched down to retrieve the empty carton, the dog suddenly walked towards Amani and licked his right hand.

"Aww, you're welcome," Amani smiled.

Sensing that it was safe to approach the canine, Amani stood up. The dog started to jump on Amani, its tail wagging. It was a completely different animal. What a smart move! Amani figured the best way to calm an angry dog is with food. He began to loosen the leash from around the fence it was tied to.

"Hey! That's my dog!" someone shouted.

Amani looked to his left and saw a man walking up the street. The dog turned to the man and began growling and barking.

"I'm sorry. I didn't know..." Amani began, but the ferocity of the dog's barking cut him off. The canine was out of control.

The man started running towards Amani. Amani realized the pooch wanted nothing to do with this man for whatever reason. He had to save this dog!

Amani completely loosened the leash, picked the dog up and began running in the other direction.

"Hey! Come back here with my dog!" yelled the man.

Amani continued running until he arrived at his driveway. He ran to the backyard to hide. The dog was panting heavily.

"You gotta keep quiet," Amani whispered.

He listened for any sounds from the man who was chasing him. After a few minutes, all remained quiet. He put the dog down and proceeded to tie the leash to the fence of his next-door neighbor.

"Stay here for a moment," Amani said as he petted the dog. "I'm going to open the back door and let you into the basement."

To get to the back door, however, Amani had to return the same way he came out. He reached for the rope, still hanging from the window. He gave it a hard tug and began to climb the wall.

Amani carefully worked his way up the wall looking back at times to make sure the dog was safe. Both animal and boy were watching each other at this point, the dog probably amazed at seeing Amani climb up the side of a house.

As Amani neared the window, he turned his attention back to his destination. With one long pull Amani was able to grab the windowsill with his left hand. He let the rope go with his right hand and placed it on the window and pulled himself up.

"Amani?" a voice whispered.

Amani's eyes widened. He was in the middle of pulling his body through the window when he froze in place.

"What are you doing?" The voice continued.

Amani looked through the window into the room and saw his little sister Sandy staring back at him in all his costumed glory.

He was caught.

END OF BOOK 1

ABOUT THE AUTHORS

Jamiyl Samuels has been creatively writing for over 25 years. Whether it is screenwriting, making numerous contributions to entertainment magazines, blogs and websites as a freelance writer, creating poetry or song lyrics, Samuels continues to do what he loves while striving to make an impact with his work.

He began his college career as a Theatre major at **Morgan State University** in the fall of 1996. He graduated with a Bachelors degree in English and a Masters degree in Media Arts with a concentration in screenwriting from **Long Island University** in Brooklyn, New York.

Tracy-Ann Samuels serves as an ambassador for Autism Speaks and spearheaded the idea to turn *"The Amazingly Awesome Amani"* into a series of children's books. She aims to spread awareness about Autism through literature and community outreach via in-school readings, panel discussions, and speaking to patrons at festivals and book fairs.

She earned her Bachelors degree in Psychology and her Masters degree in Social Work from **New York University.** She has 19 years of experience in the Social Services field. As a **Senior Advisor** at New York City Children's Services, she works with children who are Developmentally Delayed, Seriously Emotionally Disturbed, and Medically Fragile.

They are the founders of W.R.E.a.C Havoc Enterprises, a company that fosters growth, creativity and education through informed written content, film, and recorded music.

They are currently working on expanding the children's book series and growing their small business online. They reside in New York with their two children.

ABOUT THE ILLUSTRATOR

Israel Ramirez is a self-taught artist who discovered he could create his thoughts in illustrated form from the early age of five.

Although his love for illustration and cartooning was great, he found himself devoting more time to sports and church. This led to an approximate period of almost 18 years where art was not his primary focus.

Now a father and blue-collar worker, his passion to create art reignited back in 2012 upon seeing friends he grew up with, creating conversation-worthy illustrations.

Currently, Ramirez can be found on social media making logos and helping entrepreneurs and startups create their brand identity, as well as creating politically charged caricatures and other humorous topics.

Follow Israel Ramirez on Instagram **@theuncredible**

www.ingramcontent.com/pod-product-compliance
Lightning Source LLC
LaVergne TN
LVHW010025070426

835509LV00001B/10